LAMBORGHINI

T0394957

BY DALTON RAINS

Apex is distributed by North Star Editions:
sales@northstareditions.com | 888-417-0195

Produced for Apex by Red Line Editorial.

Photographs ©: Pexels, cover; iStockphoto, 1, 10–11, 12–13, 16–17; Shutterstock Images, 4–5, 14, 20, 23, 24, 25, 26–27, 29; Martyn Lucy/Getty Images News/Getty Images, 6–7; Jeff Gilbert/Alamy, 9; National Motor Museum/Heritage Images/Hulton Archive/Getty Images, 18–19; Matt Jelonek/Getty Images News/Getty Images, 21; Zoonar GmbH/Kitch Bain/Alamy, 22–23

Library of Congress Control Number: 2025930290

ISBN
979-8-89250-522-2 (hardcover)
979-8-89250-558-1 (paperback)
979-8-89250-629-8 (ebook pdf)
979-8-89250-594-9 (hosted ebook)

Printed in the United States of America
Mankato, MN
082025

NOTE TO PARENTS AND EDUCATORS

Apex books are designed to build literacy skills in striving readers. Exciting, high-interest content attracts and holds readers' attention. The text is carefully leveled to allow students to achieve success quickly. Additional features, such as bolded glossary words for difficult terms, help build comprehension.

TABLE OF CONTENTS

CHAPTER 1

SPEED TEST

A driver slams down on the gas pedal. He's testing the Lamborghini Revuelto. The tires of the **supercar** screech. The car shoots down a track.

In 2024, a Lamborghini Revuelto cost more than $500,000.

The Lamborghini is an orange blur. Its engine roars. The car keeps accelerating. It goes faster and faster. The driver is pushed back in his seat.

EVEN MORE POWER

The Lamborghini Revuelto came out in 2023. The **hybrid** sports car had three electric motors. These motors added even more speed to its **V12** engine.

The Revuelto's electric motors help the car regain speed after turns.

The **speedometer** quickly shoots past 60 miles per hour (97 km/h). It took less than three seconds. The Revuelto is Lamborghini's most powerful model yet.

FAST FACT

The Lamborghini Revuelto has a top speed of about 218 miles per hour (351 km/h).

Regular cars have about 200 horsepower. The Revuelto can reach 1,001. ▶

CHAPTER 2

HISTORY

n the 1960s, Ferruccio Lamborghini started a car company. He wanted to make better cars than Ferrari. His first car came out in 1964. It was called the 350 GT.

Ferruccio Lamborghini had a tractor company before he came out with the 350 GT.

The Miura came out in 1966. It was Lamborghini's first supercar. The Miura had a top speed of 174 miles per hour (280 km/h). It had a smooth, **streamlined** body.

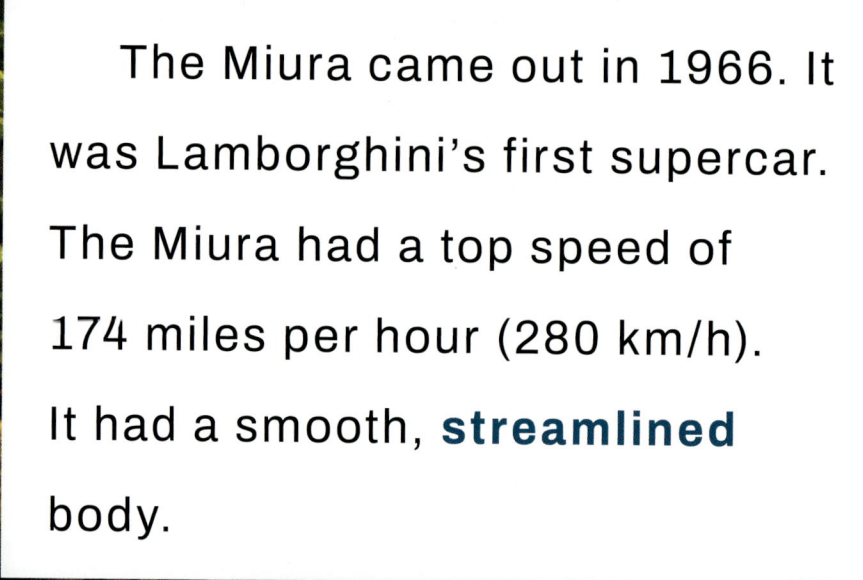

FIGHTING BULLS

Ferruccio Lamborghini visited Don Eduardo Miura in 1962. Miura's family raised fighting bulls. Lamborghini named the Miura after them. And many later Lamborghini names were related to bullfighting.

The Miura was the fastest road-legal car when it was released.

The first Countach arrived in 1974. The car had sharp corners. They gave the car a wedge shape. People loved the look. Today, many supercars have a similar shape.

FAST FACT

The Diablo was the first Lamborghini supercar with all-wheel drive.

◀ **The Countach was the first road-legal car with scissor doors.**

CHAPTER 3

MODERN LAMBORGHINIS

S tarting in the 2000s, Lamborghini sold two kinds of sports cars. A higher-end line had V12 engines. A less expensive line used V10s or V8s instead.

Lamborghini sold more than 14,000 V10 Gallardos.

The Murciélago was Lamborghini's first new car in 11 years.

Murciélagos sold from 2001 to 2010. Their V12 engines roared with power. The V10 Gallardo came out in 2003. Both models were huge hits.

FAST FACT

In 2002, the Murciélago traveled a record-setting 189.5 miles (305 km) in one hour.

Lamborghini sold more Aventadors than all of its older V12 cars put together.

In the 2010s, Lamborghini released the V12 Aventador and V10 Huracán. Fighter jets **inspired** their **designs**. Then, the V12 Revuelto and V8 Temerario arrived in the 2020s.

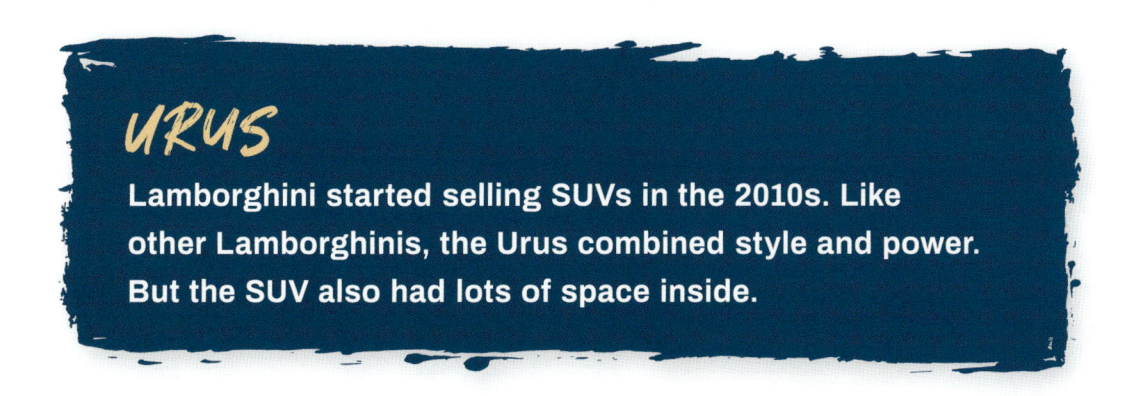

URUS

Lamborghini started selling SUVs in the 2010s. Like other Lamborghinis, the Urus combined style and power. But the SUV also had lots of space inside.

The Temerario was Lamborghini's first V8 car since the 1980s.

CHAPTER 4

RARE MODELS

Lamborghini made several other models during the 2000s. The Reventón was released in 2007. Only 35 of them were built.

The Reventón's look was based on F-22 Raptor fighter jets.

The starting price for the Sesto Elemento was about $2.6 million.

The Sesto Elemento came out in 2010. Its **carbon fiber** body made it very light. And the car could go from 0 to 60 miles per hour (0 to 97 km/h) in 2.5 seconds.

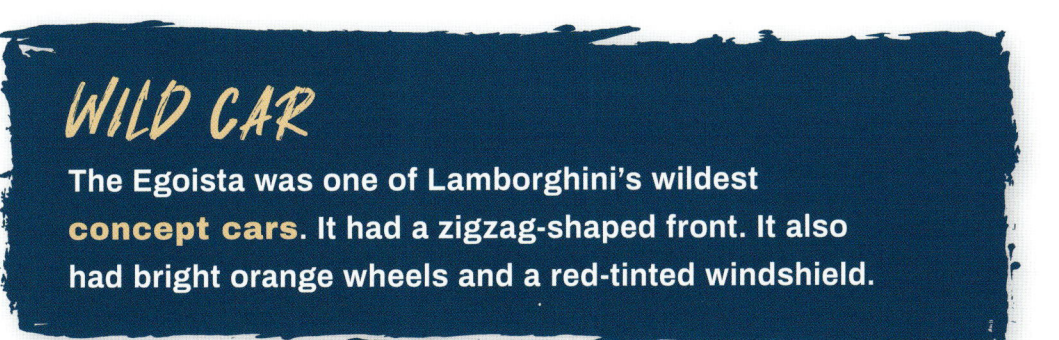

WILD CAR

The Egoista was one of Lamborghini's wildest **concept cars**. It had a zigzag-shaped front. It also had bright orange wheels and a red-tinted windshield.

The designer of the Egoista said it was meant to look like a UFO on wheels.

2010

2014

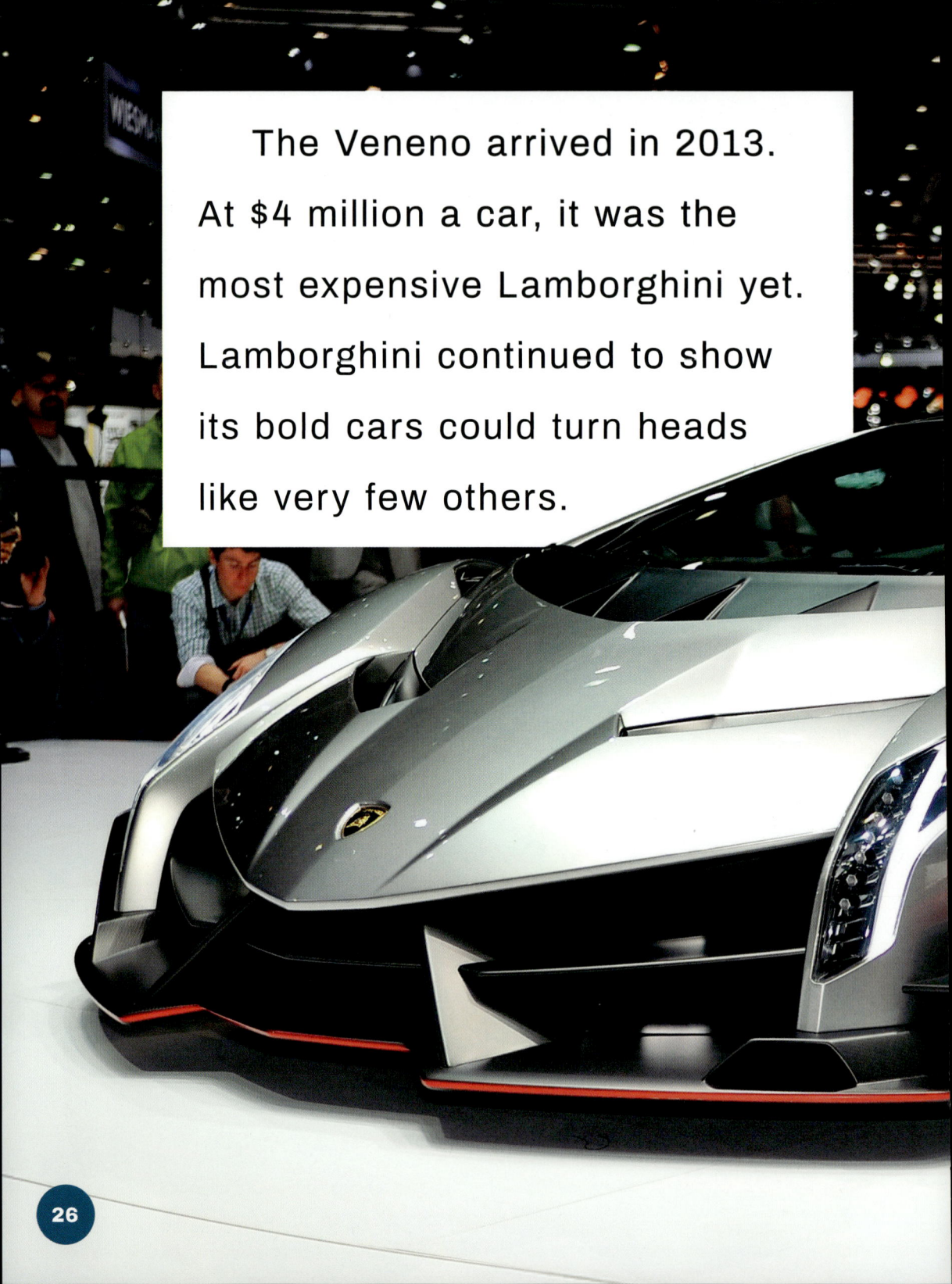

The Veneno arrived in 2013. At $4 million a car, it was the most expensive Lamborghini yet. Lamborghini continued to show its bold cars could turn heads like very few others.

The Veneno could reach speeds of 221 miles per hour (355 km/h).

COMPREHENSION
QUESTIONS

Write your answers on a separate piece of paper.

1. Write a few sentences explaining the main ideas of Chapter 2.

2. Which Lamborghini model would you most like to have? Why?

3. When did the first Lamborghini come out?

    A. 1964

    B. 1966

    C. 1974

4. What year was Ferruccio Lamborghini born?

    A. 1903

    B. 1910

    C. 1916

5. What does **accelerating** mean in this book?

*The car keeps **accelerating**. It goes faster and faster.*

    A. gaining speed

    B. losing speed

    C. stopping

6. What does **higher-end** mean in this book?

*A **higher-end** line had V12 engines. A less expensive line used V10s or V8s instead.*

    A. slower

    B. more expensive

    C. more common

Answer key on page 32.

GLOSSARY

carbon fiber
A light material that is made of thin, strong chains of carbon.

concept cars
Vehicles that show new technologies or designs.

designs
The way things look or are made.

hybrid
Able to use two different sources of energy, such as gas and electricity.

inspired
Started or gave the idea for something.

speedometer
An instrument that measures a vehicle's speed.

streamlined
Shaped to move quickly through air or water.

supercar
A car fast enough for racing that can also go on the street.

V12
A powerful, expensive engine that uses gas.

BOOKS

Duling, Kaitlyn. *Lamborghini Aventador*. Bellwether Media, 2024.

Hamilton, S. L. *Lamborghini*. Abdo Publishing, 2023.

Morey, Allan. *Inventing Cars*. Focus Readers, 2022.

ONLINE RESOURCES

Visit **www.apexeditions.com** to find links and resources related to this title.

ABOUT THE AUTHOR

Dalton Rains is a writer and editor from St. Paul, Minnesota. He would love to drive a Lamborghini someday.

INDEX

ANSWER KEY:
1. Answers will vary; 2. Answers will vary; 3. A; 4. C; 5. A; 6. B